Ant Attack

WITHDRAWN

Anthony McGowan
Illustrated by Jon Stuart

Previously ...

In the story *Ant Storm*, Max, Cat, Ant and Tiger are forced out of their micro-den – a toy fort on an island in the pond in the park – by an army of ants.

The children set off on a micro-adventure to find out what has happened to the ants' old nest. The children find a tunnel and follow it. They have to escape a hungry mole along the way.

At the end of the tunnel, they are shocked to find that the ants' nest has been taken over by X-bots! It has been transformed into an X-bot factory – where some new, scary ant-bots are in charge.

One of the ant-bots catches the children unawares and fires a net out towards them …

Meanwhile, in his NASTI hideout, Dr X is about to switch on to see what's happening in his new factory.

3

The net shot out from the ant-bot and sailed towards the micro-friends. It looked like they were all going to be captured.

Max thought fast. "MOVE!" he yelled.

He gave Ant a shove, pushing him beyond the reach of the net. Tiger dived into a forward roll, out of the way.

Max and Cat, however, were well and truly snared. The net was as sticky as chewing-gum.

"Get out of here, you two!" Max shouted. "Keep your watches safe!"

Tiger and Ant did not want to leave their friends behind. But then the giant ant-bot turned to them. It was getting ready to fire another net.

"Go!" said Cat, in her fiercest voice. She was trying to cover up just how frightened she was.

Chapter 2 – Split!

Tiger was nearest the ant-bot. It reared up and fired the second net. Tiger ducked just in time and the net splattered into the wall behind him. The ant-bot hissed in anger. There was only one way out for Tiger – back along the tunnel, the way they had come.

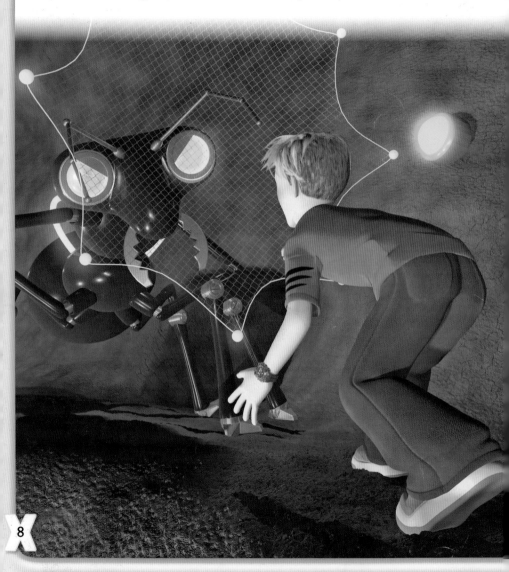

Not stopping to think, Tiger threw himself forwards – diving between the legs of the terrifying new X-bot. He skidded out the other side, quickly picked himself up and sprinted off down the tunnel. He flicked the light on his watch on as he ran. His stomach was churning. He felt sick about leaving his friends behind.

Ant, meanwhile, had dashed in the opposite direction. He followed the ledge that ran round the chamber of the old ants' nest. He was aiming for another tunnel that Max had spotted earlier. It led, he hoped, out into the fresh air and to safety.

The ant-bot that had netted Max and Cat made a loud bleeping noise. All the X-bots in the chamber turned to look. In a second they were scuttling to intercept the escapees.

Ant ran as fast as he could. He was almost there. It looked like he was going to make it! But, just then, two X-bots scrambled up on to the ledge to block his way. Ant tried to swerve past them. He jumped to one side but lost his footing and tumbled off the edge, down the bank of earth … towards the middle of the X-bot factory.

Cat screamed as Ant fell. She and Max had been watching his escape attempt from within the tangled, sticky threads of the net.

Their ant-bot captor clacked its jaws together angrily at the noise. It picked up the net with its front legs, dangling Max and Cat in the air. It gave the net a quick, spiteful shake and then brought it close up to its wicked eyes.

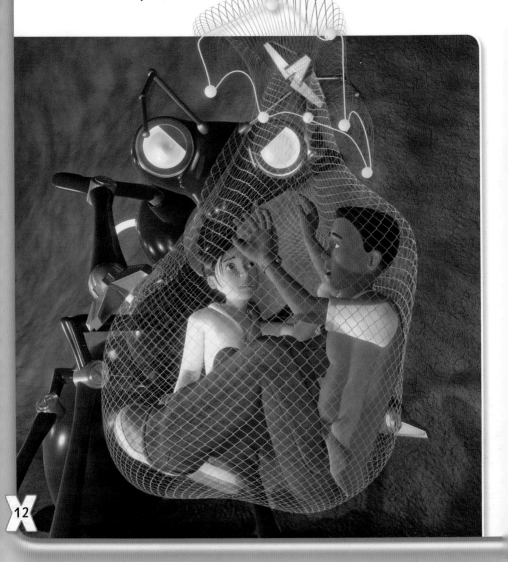

Ant finally rolled to a stop. Once his head had stopped spinning, he saw that he had landed in front of the big, gleaming machine for assembling the X-bots. All the different pieces went in on a conveyor belt on one side, and the X-bots emerged fully assembled from the other side.

Behind him, Ant heard a noise – a loud metallic hissing and snapping. Slowly, he turned round to see a semicircle of ant-bot guards closing in on him. One of them took a step forwards. Ant stifled a scream.

There was only one way Ant could go. Keeping his eyes fixed on the ant-bots in front of him, he moved backwards, feeling his way, and carefully climbed up on to the machine.

The ant-bots moved towards him. Ant looked from them to the gaping mouth of the machine. He had no choice.

"Here goes nothing," he said to himself.

With that, he turned and sprinted forwards … into the machine. Behind him the X-bots screeched angrily.

Ant was surrounded by assembly machines each putting different parts of X-bots together. Some assembled the leg sections. Others assembled the heads. Others worked on the bodies. At the end, all the sections were joined together.

Ant looked up. He could see only one way out – at the top of the machine. His heart filled with hope.

Ant jumped up on to the conveyor belt and ran along it. It was exhausting as he had to run at double speed because the conveyor belt was moving in the opposite direction. He also had to dodge the assembly machines that were putting the parts of the X-bots together.

Chapter 4 – Tiger's tunnel surprise

Tiger could hear the scuttling footsteps of the pursuing X-bots behind him. He looked back over his shoulder and saw the green lights from their eyes. They were almost on him. Sweat poured down his face. He tried to concentrate, but he kept thinking about Max and Cat trapped in the net. He knew he had to rescue them. But how?

Then the answer came to him. Or rather, it *hit* him. Or, rather still, he hit *it*.

SMACK!

Tiger ran straight into the back of something soft and furry. He heard a low, angry grunt.

"Aaarrrggghhhhhhhhhh!" he screamed, when it turned to face him. It was the mole that he and the others had been chased by when they were trying to find the ants' nest.

The mole turned round. It was annoyed. Very annoyed. And still hungry. The mole made another grunt and lunged at Tiger.

Chapter 5 – Dangling

"What do you think they're going to do with us?" asked Cat.

Max and Cat were hanging from a hook over the X-bot factory floor.

"I'm not sure. I guess they'll take us to Dr X."

"I wonder why they haven't done that already?"

"I don't think they were expecting us. This place is obviously designed to produce a new X-bot army. They didn't think we'd come blundering in here, bringing the watches right to them. They'll inform Dr X about us soon, and then … well, let's just hope Ant or Tiger can think of something."

Ant had almost made it through the machine. Then, just as he was about to jump down from the conveyor belt, he tripped. The belt dragged him back through the line of assembly bots.

Ant looked up to see the head of an X-bot descending towards him. He couldn't get out of the way. He screamed and darkness fell.

The X-bot head felt heavy. Ant tried to pull it off, but it was stuck. He looked out and felt a bit sick … he could see the world exactly as an X-bot would see it.

"I feel like an insect," he thought.

That gave him an idea.

Ant let the conveyor belt carry him out of the machine. He jumped down and ran out along the tunnel. With the X-bot head on, the guards did not recognize him as an intruder and did not stop him.

Ant made his way back to the opening of the tunnel at the base of the tree in the park. Then he climbed carefully along the branch that led back to the island in the pond.

The island was now full of worker ants. They had the queen and her brood to look after, and they were busy foraging for food.

Ant went straight to the fort. He hoped his plan would work. It was the only way he could think of rescuing Max and Cat before they were taken to NASTI.

Chapter 7 – Ant's crazy plan

The main doorway to the fort was protected by two scary-looking soldier ants. There was no way he was going to be able to get past them.

Quickly, he ran round the back where there was a secret entrance. Luckily, the ants had not found it and it was not guarded.

He snuck into the fort and began searching. In one of the towers, he found the brood chamber. This was where the eggs and baby ants were cared for. Without pausing, Ant carefully picked up two of the soft ant grubs and ran towards the main gates. He barged past the guards and ran off.

When the queen ant saw what had happened, she issued her commands. An army of workers and soldiers marched after Ant, in order to save the babies from what they thought was a fierce predator.

Ant made his way back along the branch towards the tunnel. The ants were not far behind. He knew that he would come to a sticky end if they caught him.

Meanwhile ...

Back at NASTI, Socket noticed a sign flashing on a monitor.

"Boss, there's a message coming in from the new factory."

Dr X waved him away. "It can wait," he replied, reaching for another slice of the cake. "Even evil geniuses are allowed to have a few minutes off on their birthday, aren't they?"

"Yes, boss," sighed Plug and Socket, still eyeing the rapidly dwindling cake.

Chapter 8 – Ant attack!

Max breathed a sigh of relief. He and Cat had been watching the X-bots as they tried to get through to NASTI. They didn't seem to be having much luck.

"That doesn't mean they won't get through in a minute," Cat pointed out.

"You're right. If only we had something we could use to cut through this net!" he said desperately.

Cat was absently picking at a loose strand of the netting.

"Umm," she said. "Max, how about we use this …?" She pulled the strand and a long thread came free.

"Cat, how are we going to escape with that?" he sighed.

"Like this," she said. She wrapped the thread round part of the netting, held each end and began to saw it back and forward.

One by one, the strands began to fray and then ping apart.

"Cat, you're a genius!"

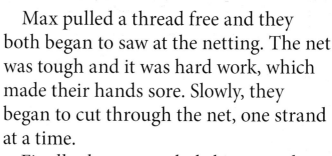

Max pulled a thread free and they both began to saw at the netting. The net was tough and it was hard work, which made their hands sore. Slowly, they began to cut through the net, one strand at a time.

Finally there was a hole big enough in the net for them to break through.

Max hoped to burst out, catching the X-bots by surprise.

"On the count of three," he whispered. One, two, thr –"

Before he could finish, a wild commotion broke out in the factory.

Suddenly there were black ants everywhere. Angry ants! And right in the middle of them, was a very strange X-bot. It had the head of an X-bot, but the body of …

"Ant!" cried Cat.

Ant had led the ants right to the factory. He ran straight to the machine and put the grubs he had taken from the brood chamber in the fort on to the conveyor belt. The ants swarmed after them, wanting to protect them, and the X-bots swarmed after the ants. A desperate fight began.

The battle raged on. The ants' jaws were not much use against the metal X-bots. But when they squirted formic acid, the X-bots fizzled and fizzed and then shut down.

However, there were more X-bots than there were ants, and one by one they picked up the ants and threw them out of their old nest. Soon the battle would be over and once again the X-bots would have control of their factory.

"Guys, guys!" came a voice from beneath Max and Cat.

They looked down at the latest Ant-bot.

"What –" began Max.

But Ant cut him off. "There's no time to explain now but –"

And then the net broke and Max and Cat fell in a heap on top of Ant.

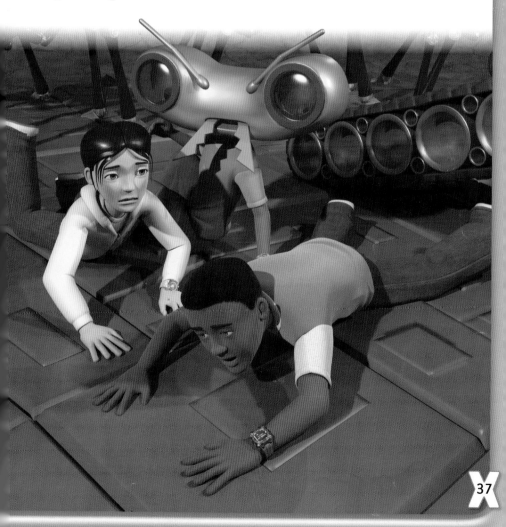

An ant-bot guard turned to face them. It looked down and clicked its jaws together angrily. It got ready to fire another net. But it never got the chance. For at that moment, Tiger came tearing out of the tunnel.

Right behind him charged the enraged mole. It paused for a moment, as it found itself in this new space, sniffing the air hungrily. But then it got to work. It lashed out with its powerful front paws, sending X-bots flying in all directions. Its sharp teeth crunched through the X-bots as if they were peanuts.

The ant-bot that had been guarding Max and Cat went to join the battle.

"Over here, Tiger!" Max yelled.

Tiger dashed over to the others. He nearly ran away again when he saw Ant.

"It's only me," said Ant. "And don't you dare say a word," he warned, when he saw Tiger's lips begin to curl into a smile.

"Let's get out of here," said Max. "We can have the explanations later."

The micro-friends ran towards the tunnel. The X-bots were too busy fighting both the ants and the mole to bother them.

Ant, however, stopped and turned back. "I just need a moment," he said. He ran back into the X-bot-making machine.

"I think that X-bot head has sent him a bit funny," said Tiger. "What's he up to?"

Ant was only in the machine for a couple of seconds before he joined his friends again.

They soon reached the fresh air at the end of the tunnel. It was only then that Tiger had the chance for a proper laugh at Ant.

"You don't make a very scary X-bot," he gasped.

Ant started laughing, too.

"Come on," said Max, "let's get you out of that thing."

Max, Cat and Tiger together managed to pull Ant's X-bot head off. Then all four children turned the dials on their watches. They pushed the X ... and grew back to normal size.

"I think I'll keep this as a souvenir," said Ant, holding up the now tiny X-bot head he had been wearing.

They watched the entrance to the ants' nest. There was a grinding, crashing noise, and little pieces of X-bot flew out of the hole, followed by a puff of black smoke.

"What on earth was that?" Cat asked.

"Oh, I pushed the lever to send the conveyor belt into reverse in that X-bot machine. I guessed it would probably wreck it."

"Well done!" said Max. "And thanks to both of you for coming back to rescue us. It was a great idea to use the ants like that, Ant."

"Yes," said Cat, admiringly. "And it was really brilliant of you, Tiger, to lure the mole back there."

Tiger blushed. "Yes, well, it was nothing …"

In fact, Tiger hadn't really had a plan at all. He was just running away from the mole!

As they watched, they saw more ants, led by their queen, returning to the nest.

"Looks like the ants have won," said Max.

"And we have got our fort back," said Tiger.

"Great," said Cat. "We should celebrate."

"And I think I know how," said Ant, smiling. "After all, this whole adventure began when that ant ate my ice cream!"

Meanwhile ...

Back at NASTI HQ, Dr X had finally finished all of his birthday cake. He was now in a very good mood.

"Right, now let's see what that message from the new production facility was all about."

Find out more ...

For another exciting adventure read *Round-up*.

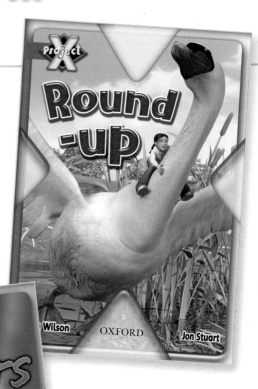

Find out how animals survive in the wild in *Animal Conflicts*.